There is hardly anybody on th[
spiritual depths of the Enneagram, as does Suzanne Zuercher!
Her constant insights are grounded, not just in good psychology
and good theology, but also with an uncanny grasp of the bril-
liance of this spiritual tool. She represents the depths that the
Enneagram came from and the depths where it can lead you.

Fr. Richard Rohr, O.F.M.
Center for Action and Contemplation, Albuquerque, New
Mexico

In a masterly way, Sr. Suzanne guides the reader toward
understanding how a one-sidedness of seeing comes with each
Enneagram space and especially how people's personalities
affect the way they pray. This book has significantly helped
me to recognize how I, with my personality, can cooperate
better with God's grace, as well as to assist others in such
cooperation.

Fr. Thomas Leitner, O.S.B.
St. Benedict Center, Schuyler, Nebraska

Suzanne Zuercher has a way of getting to the most central
notion and heart of the spiritual journey: contemplative life.
She knows how to awaken in spiritual seekers the longing to
be at home in the very personality that God has gifted them
with by opening to the reader the deepest meaning of the
Enneagram. *Using the Enneagram in Prayer* is an invitation for
entering into the core of this lifetime pilgrimage into God
through the insights and wisdom of the Enneagram. Suzanne
offers a refreshing perspective of this ancient path for a contemporary life, and if we but learn to "hold lightly" this delicate

offering it will be a feast for the soul of the one who desires to live life closer to the true self/Spirit self abiding in the deepest dimensions of our being. An excellent help for those spiritual directors, directees, and those who guide the spiritual journey of others.

Nancy Brousseau, O.P.
Director, Dominican (Spirituality) Center at Marywood

What a treasure this book is for all who minister in the field of spirituality, spiritual direction, and retreats. Clearly Suzanne is steeped in both the Enneagram and in a profound, seasoned knowledge and understanding of our human/God journey. Thus, in clear understandable language, she gives a tool for moving into our own inner truth and companioning others who invite us to walk with them on their journey.

Rita Lui, O.P.
Director, Racine Dominican Retreat Program at Siena Center, Racine, Wisconsin

USING THE

ENNEAGRAM

IN PRAYER

A CONTEMPLATIVE GUIDE

SUZANNE ZUERCHER

AVE MARIA PRESS AVE Notre Dame, Indiana

© 2008 by Suzanne Zuercher, O.S.B.

Founded in 1865, Ave Maria Press is a ministry of the United States Province of Holy Cross.

www.avemariapress.com

ISBN-10 1-59471-173-9 ISBN-13 978-1-59471-173-2

Cover and text design by Brian C. Conley.

Printed and bound in the United States of America.

Library of Congress Cataloging-in-Publication Data
Zuercher, Suzanne.
Using the enneagram in prayer : a contemplative guide / Suzanne Zuercher.
       p. cm.
Includes bibliographical references.
ISBN-13: 978-1-59471-173-2 (pbk.)
ISBN-10: 1-59471-173-9 (pbk.)
1. Prayer–Christianity. 2. Enneagram. I. Title.
BV215.Z84 2008
248.3–dc22

2008002375

CONTENTS

PREFACE

For more than thirty years the Enneagram has been for me a source of insight about my self and other people. Early on I recognized that it was far more than a mere personality description, a mere typology. I struggled for some time to describe the significance this system assumed in my personal life and work. Eventually I found the words I was looking for: The Enneagram is a spiritual Way.

Its unclear origin, shrouded in history, has always emphasized our deepest selves where we incarnate some aspect of the Divine at our core and center. The Enneagram also speaks about the ways that, depending on our stance in life, our fear leads us to distort this initial giftedness. The free and open channel of life the

Creator intended each of us to be in the building up of creation becomes compromised very early. As conscious human beings, we need to admit and face this loss, to correct the fearful distrust of a loving environment that encouraged us to create our defensive ego. Then we can address the ways we learned, depending on our unique stance in life, to protect ourselves from ourselves, others, the environment, and God. Armed with this knowledge, we can grow in the freedom that allows us to fulfill our human destiny.

Of course, there are other ways to come to such awareness, but the Enneagram has been for me the clearest and most helpful. It speaks articulately about this human condition, this sense that we are not only unloved but unlovable, that we must survive on our own by creating layers of defenses. This condition is called by theologians our "original sin." The Enneagram assists us on the journey toward mature wholeness by describing the life themes of the nine personalities and the issues encountered along each path to wholeness.

This present volume is a natural step in the development of these ideas. It has been asked for by people who are searching for a way to touch their deeper selves and open in trust and love to life/Life, both personal and Divine. Another way to put this would be to say that they are looking for ways to return to the freedom of the children of God. While the book assumes basic knowledge of Enneagram theory, I will briefly summarize here the framework from which I personally view its contribution.

Let me begin by saying that all aspects of creation, not only the creation of human beings, are said to have nine different manifestations. When applied to human beings, which is our interest here, a number is assigned to each of the nine stances. For me, a helpful image of this theory is that of a prism of light. As one color in a prism gradually shades into the next, so the nine kinds of personality merge from one to another around this circular figure representing the totality of human creation. These nine stances or gestures or spaces into which the human race is incarnated, group into triads: the 8/9/1 people are called the feelers, the 2/3/4 people are called the doers or imitators, and the 5/6/7 people are called the perceivers or observers.

Each of these triads faces different issues along the way to conversion, or individuation, or transformation—however one chooses to name the movement toward wholeness.

A Basic Outline of the 8/9/1 Triad

The intense emotional response of the 8/9/1s is what frightens them more than anything else. The first person they feel they need to control is the one within. This they try to do by answering their own emotional response with reason and logic. Depending on the individual space among the three, 8/9/1s either consciously try to curb their emotions by an organized, rational defense or else fail altogether even to allow feelings in, but rather stuff them away out of their awareness. The pseudo-logic they use is based on a premise of liking or not liking; around this initial instinctive judgment a seemingly objective case in defense of their subjective prejudgment builds up.

The varying emotions of 8/9/1s are frequently converted into anger, something at least familiar to them, though not necessarily pleasant. These people instinctively hold their ground rather than adapt to people and circumstances. They struggle with where their own boundaries and those of others begin and end. They sometimes feel they are drowning in the emotional intensity of the moment. Consequently, they find the present all they can deal with. They tend to forget the hassles and battles of the past and often bury their former issues, carrying them along as part of the burden of the present. When the passion of the moment, be it emotional or physical, becomes too strong, they see themselves as "bad," which means out of control or less than human. They fear that deep in their human nature they are flawed beyond redemption.

To cover over that fear, this triad needs to feel strong, and this means being in control of themselves as well as decisive in relationships with other. They are concerned with power and strive to win the battles of life over self and other people. They are often assertive and either actively or passively aggressive, either imposing their will or holding their ground and refusing to let anyone take it away.

Their question in life is "Who am I?" Many people ask the same question at one or another time, but in this triad it highlights a major concern over parameters and limits. When tides of emotions rise between themselves and others in relationships or blind their thinking around causes in which they are involved, 8/9/1s can find their personal boundaries washed away. This experience is the other side of—and possibly the reason for—strong self-preservation instincts. Conservation of energy, of time, of involvement are attempts to keep their individual person from being merged with all the rest of their experience.

A Basic Outline of the 2/3/4 Triad

This doer or imitative triad moves into activity instinctively. They tend to turn their emotions into anxiety, a feeling that keeps them in motion, and one with which they are most familiar. Fear and anger, for example, may appear first in their awareness as agitation or a mental script or scenario of future events, or something as simple as a binge of housecleaning.

Unlike the planted energy of the 8/9/1s, this triad's energy moves out into the world around them. Instinctively social, they adapt to what they think the environment and people in it want of them. As a consequence, they may not even notice their personal response to things, let alone their personal needs. They concentrate on connections among people and find the world a network of well- or not well-functioning relationships. As is true of all the triads, they assume everyone else does or should see life as they do. "Who am I with?" and "How am I doing?" are their spontaneous questions, both of which focus on life outside themselves and manifest their desire for affirmation. It is as though they carry a measuring stick by which they compare themselves to everyone else. Since they identify so strongly with what they are doing, to come up short in their own or other people's eyes is to fail in life. They look to control, to stay on top of their lives, by getting things done, by having something to show, some product for their efforts.

This triad often discounts and lacks the experience of living in the present. Good or bad old times color their reminiscence and cause nostalgia for the past. Plans and tasks and figuring out what to do take them ahead in time. Consequently, the present seems to have no reality; it is only a small crack that separates past from future.

2/3/4s look like emotional people, either cheerful and friendly or heavy and melancholy, depending on what is called for by the environment. Actually, they have a hard time allowing into their experience and expressing to other people their inner feelings. Their real and personal emotional life seems to be missing because it is put aside in favor of that of others. Since they are so outer oriented, they imitate what others are feeling and what the circumstances around them call for. Their own inner experience is crowded out by these distractions from others, and they rarely take the time to stop and discover their own experience.

A Basic Outline of the 5/6/7 Triad

This triad's energy is one which takes data from the outer world into a safe, interior place where they can be arranged into something meaningful. These people search for order inside that will protect them from threat outside, and they look for where they fit into the scheme of things. While they may see many possibilities of what might be done, these options often remain merely ideas and are never turned into anything concrete. Because they tend to wait so long to be sure they have enough information, they often feel forgotten and overlooked. Life and the people in it go on past, leaving them behind, attempting to figure things out.

Fear is the prominent emotion in this triad, and fear tends to paralyze. Consequently, actions do not flow naturally as the fruit of their perceptions. Taking in sensory stimuli and ideas, ordering these, and imagining possibilities or consequences flowing from them receive their attention and emphasis. Getting it together in their minds is what gives them a feeling of control. Because there is always more one can learn, 5/6/7 reality tends to remain an inner one, and these people have a hard time moving to decisions which can then lead them into action.

The issue for this triad is "rightness." Where does new information fit into an already created inner schema of reality? This is a question of consonance with some inner construct or map. It does not have a flavor of morality as it would have for the 8/9/1s who view life in terms of good or bad. The inner search for a new whole that incorporates additional information is what often accounts for the 5/6/7 sense of being lost and confused and for their question: "Where am I?"

The emotions of 5/6/7s are what help them link perception to action. When they experience the resonance of their feelings in their bodies, they discover that their energy has been engaged, and then they are empowered to act with sureness and courage. Such visibility is a mixed blessing for 5/6/7s. On the one hand they are no longer uncertain and forgotten; on the other they lose a privacy and anonymity they treasure and long to preserve.

Summary

This very brief outline of the three Enneagram triads may give you some sense of your personal dynamics. On the other hand, because it is so limited, it may not. There is much more to be said about the basic incarnated stances or life gestures, the motivations and the behaviors of not only the triads, but each space within each triad. I have hardly touched on the significance of the gift each kind of person offers to creation. Neither have I spoken much about how these differing ways of looking at creation affect one's view of the Creator of Life, one's own and that of others who inhabit this world. If you are not familiar with Enneagram theory, I trust that you will take the well-spent time to go more deeply into such a study. I recommend the writings of A.H. Almaas and Sandra Maitri as what I consider the best articulations of this spiritual dimension. You will find their works referenced in the following chapters.

Most of all, I encourage those who have not yet done so to participate in workshops where people who live in each of these spaces speak about their joys and sorrows, their issues and problems, their pitfalls and distortions of reality. There is no better way to learn the Enneagram than to observe the various energies incarnated in human beings and to listen to their stories. This is an oral tradition, and its study is best initiated in a setting where people share their lives.

I assume here that my readers possess such a background. If that is not the case, I hope this introduction, limited though it is, will encourage them to seek out such opportunities. The more extensive one's knowledge of the Enneagram, the more relevant will be the following suggestions for what can assist a person along the spiritual path.

This having been said, there is also much in the book that speaks of an attitude of contemplation, a gift that is meant for all human beings, whoever they may be. Knowledge of the Enneagram, while useful, is not absolutely necessary for those discussions. While I have found that the Enneagram clarifies issues that make contemplation difficult, the pages that follow will, I hope, still have relevance with or without knowledge of this system.

All of us are called to be contemplative. This is the most important truth I hope readers remember from this book. As conscious beings, we are called to share our lives with the One Who Is Without Limit. This is our marvelous vocation and one which will lead us to maturity and the fullness of our human destiny.

INTRODUCTION

This book is about the person who prays, and that pray-er looked at from the perspective of the Enneagram. It is not primarily about prayers, but rather it is intended to help people find the place within themselves where they meet their spirit, and in doing so meet also the Divine Spirit. Finding this presence to Presence constitutes the spiritual life, the contemplative life, the full human life, the life of the pray-er, the life of prayer.

Over the years I have noticed the very limited view many people have of the life of prayer. People often view prayer as something separate from the rest of their lives. Its boundaries of time and place set it apart from everything else, which then becomes non-prayer.

This concept of non-prayer usually gets enlarged to one of non-spiritual, non-sacred, or secular. Life divides into opposites in this area as in so many others. On the one side there is the holy. On the other is what at best we call non-holy and at worst, un-holy. These divisions result in a rigid and static view of life. Prayer in this formulation is often reduced to a dialogue with our current projection of the Divine. If we are not talking to whoever we see God to be, we say we are not praying.

Over a lifetime the One Who Is Without Limit inspires different metaphors depending on changes in the life of the pray-er. In this book I would like to focus on the pray-er that one is rather than the prayers that one says. I suggest that the Enneagram can be a help in this process, since it talks about differing people; and, viewed contemplatively, it increasingly opens up reality to the people who study it.

As Thomas Merton, a great spiritual writer of the twentieth century, got older he became more and more reluctant to talk about prayer. He discovered, as he grew wiser and more whole, that there is no need to knock on the door to get into God's presence. We are, indeed, already there.[1] To develop a life of prayer, a life of contemplation, is the simple task of recognizing that we cannot be out of God's presence. All human beings are meant to be contemplative, whether they farm the land or work in factories, offices, or laboratories; whether they teach in universities or pre-schools or care for homes and families. All human beings are created to be conscious and aware, to look with wide open eyes at reality. Ever increasing awareness is the human being's destiny. It is this ability to reflect on creation—our own personal creation and that of other people and the world around us—that separates us from the beloved pet that sleeps beside our chair.

We are born with a contemplative bent. Just look at any small child taken up into life, and you will know that is true. Observe a child in some form of activity, be it playing a game or examining a butterfly, and you will see someone enthralled with experience. Along the way of life, however, we lose our innate ability to receive all of life that any given moment holds out to us. We become cautious, separate, distant. We build up boundaries between ourselves and the reality within and around us.

Later on, we need to re-learn the pathway to the fullness of our personal existence, of who we are. As we do this, we let in more of what is outside and around us as well. We discover as adults what we forgot in the time of growing up. We find again a receptive child, and in doing so we reclaim the contemplative attitude necessary to become a pray-er.

I would like to share some analogies that describe this contemplative attitude. One such analogy is that of friendship with ourselves. The people who are dear to us in our lives we treat with respect and reverence. We trust those people; we believe in their goodness and their respect for us. We listen to our friends when they talk to us, listen to all they have to say without cutting them off or finishing their communications because we have already decided what their message will be. An attitude of contemplation toward our lives leads us to welcome into consciousness whatever presents itself to us. We listen fully, and we listen well. We do not assume we know all there is to know about ourselves or another person or our environment. Newness and surprise are part of every friendship that remains vital, including this one with our selves.

Patience is important in friendship. We do not demand that our friends tell us everything; we wait until our friend is ready, until that friend's time. There is no hurry. We have a lifetime together, and some communications can wait. So, too, when we have a friendly attitude toward our own lives. We invite reality into consciousness, but we do not force it in. As our own friend, we intuitively know what we can bear to hear, how much truth we are capable of handling, what it is time for.

Another image that captures for me this contemplative quality comes from Piero Ferrucci.[2] He speaks of it as holding a bird in the hand. This attitude has the "feel," if you will, of focused attention, of listening presence. We need to hold this bird, which represents our reality, with some degree of firmness. Otherwise, if we allow our thoughts to wander, they, like the bird, will escape. The discipline of listening is essential to contemplation, and that is what distinguishes it from mere daydreaming. On the other hand, this focus on whatever reality the moment presents to us, be it some feeling, person, action, or idea, cannot be too intense. Force and strain will kill the awareness as surely as a tight grasp will kill the bird we hold in our hand. Firmness and lightness, seriousness and playfulness, will keep the reality of the moment alive.

Our friendship with our selves, our truth, will prosper in such a contemplative environment. We will gradually learn from the child within us what a lifetime of denial and overlook, of forgetfulness, of insensitivity, superficiality, excessive self-scrutiny, and self-judgment led us to forget.

This attitude of honesty, of humble truth, is the cornerstone of the spiritual life. Major traditions of spirituality center in the reality of creatureliness and limitation. The doctrine of Incarnation refers not only to Jesus' welcoming embrace of earthy and earthly humanity, but to the need of all of us to follow his inspiration into the depths of our own lives.

On the way to growing into greater fullness of who we are and how we are enfleshed, we encounter the Enneagram. Knowledge of our inborn stance and view of life—and of the themes and issues we face because of that unique enfleshedness—is already to change. Knowing is change in itself. Acceptance of what we come to know is to change radically, to become converted, transformed, to let go into the reality of what is so. Gradually in life we are shaped and formed into pray-ers, people who embrace God's destiny for themselves, for others, and for the world.

Thomas Merton points out that the pray-er prays as long as he or she exists and does not run away from the center of self.[3] The Enneagram helps us see how we back away from and hold ourselves up and out of our center of humble truth. It also points out to us those inborn strengths we have which assist our journey to that interior place where our spirit dwells with the Spirit of Jesus. Such an experience holds at the same time both an awareness of our spirit and beyond our spirit to an awareness of Jesus' Spirit.

St. Benedict, who founded Western monasticism in the sixth century, begins his exploration of the spiritual life with the word "Listen."[4] I borrow this exhortation from him. I encourage you, the listener, gently and reflectively, to attend to these words in an attitude reminiscent of the firmness and flexibility with which we might hold a bird in our hand. Unless we have this attitude about the contents of this book, we will go away with facts about saying prayers and methods to use during prayer periods rather than experience which reveals and describes the self as pray-er.

Another image I like to use to describe this contemplative attitude is that of a paper ball with which Japanese children sometimes play. This ball has a hole and is blown up through this hole by a person's breath. Once the ball is inflated it remains so until some aggressively jarring blow either tears the paper or forces out all the air. If the players touch it lightly, it will remain inflated and capable of being hit back and forth through an entire ball game. This is the "touch" I suggest you reach for as you read the following chapters. An aggressive pursuit of information in an effort to make one's self a better pray-er will only result in frustration. The best way to use this book contemplatively is to bring one's personal historical experience alongside what people say has revealed the pray-er they are to themselves, and lightly—almost playfully—to let one's own experience interact with theirs.

All of our experiences are unique. That being so, you may not always agree with what these people have said about themselves as pray-ers. The oral tradition of the Enneagram underlines the ever-changing and flowing quality of human life described here. It is the true contemplative within you, the deepest word you are, the inner child without lies or pretense or caution or defense who can at best lightly and playfully engage with the many people whose shared spirituality I will attempt to describe in the pages that follow. I hope this material offers something of meaning for your prayer life, for your life as pray-er.

As I have done in my other books,[5] I invite you to contribute to the growing volume of descriptive research as you interact with this material, focusing and refining it as you do so. It is this continually evolving tradition that makes the Enneagram so alive.

May you find yourself, your pray-er, either because you see yourself described here or because these words have led you to nuance or distinguish more accurately your own truth. Your contemplative inner child will know that truth. Let that child sit beside you now as we continue.

APPROACHES TO THE
INTERIOR LIFE

Approaches to the Interior Life for the 8/9/1 Triad

How do people in this triad view living the interior life, the life of the soul, the life of the spirit, the spiritual life? For 8/9/1 people, the approach to reality is simply to be, and it is that approach of "simply being" that they also bring to the life of prayer and interiority. The spiritual masters and mistresses call it just "being in prayer." Teresa of Avila, herself most probably in this triad, described such prayer as what might be termed a loving attention.[1] Prayer of loving attention involves a centering, being at the center of one's person just who and as one is in God's presence.

This form of prayer needs no thinking, no feeling, no moving, no content. Simple being is a healing, quieting, calming experience. By emptying and detaching the self from all content one comes to this centered place, this stillness, this uncluttered simplicity. This is a peaceful place, a place of joy and of grounding. In it one lets God be God. This is a prayer of union, of oneness, and of freedom. There is a nourishing kind of stillness in this form of prayer, in this attitude of interiority.

People in the 8/9/1 spaces, in place of their usual stance in life which is struggling between self and God, flesh and spirit, learn to let go of the dividing boundaries and surrender. This is a courageous prayer activity for them for there is fear to let go into God; what will happen to them if they do so? They may get swallowed up; they may disappear; they may never get back. Such fear impedes what is their natural way to pray: simply being in the present. One way they control this fear of slipping away is to become a watchful self. This watchful self acts as a control. When this self stands next to themselves, monitoring themselves, they feel less frightened about giving in to the flow of life which might obliterate the boundaries of who they are as a separate individual. In reality, there is nothing to fear. They will not become so one with the Divine that they lose their being. They bring their being to that surrender and remain themselves even as they give themselves in prayer to God. This is what they need to learn in prayer: that God does respect and value their existence.

People who are drawn to this kind of prayer often feel guilty about it. They wonder if they are doing anything. They know their own tendency to be lazy at times and to avoid interior work. They realize that they tend to just forget things that are frightening and conflictual or else too much for them to look at in any given moment. They know they can sometimes blot reality out so it is simply not there anymore. Because of this tendency, they wonder if that is what they are doing when they take time for prayer. The test for them is in the outcome of the time they spend. If it is alive and active presence that results, they know they are, indeed, praying.

A man in this space expressed such a concern to me. I asked him what he did during the time he set aside for prayer. He answered that, after he dressed in the morning and went down to the kitchen for a cup of coffee, he would bring it back to his room and sit in his comfortable chair for about an hour. His concern was that, while sitting there, he did nothing. I asked him what it was like after that hour was over. He described himself as awake and alive and ready to begin the day, to take on whatever it would offer. I encouraged him to trust that kind of energy. The outcome of his time spent each morning was to be present in the moment, something I consider to be the essence of any kind of praying.

People in the 8/9/1 triad need energy to center and quiet themselves and meet their lives awake and alert. Rather than criticizing and judging themselves, they need to give themselves to this experience. This is not the quietism that spiritual writers talk and write about. This is neither inertia nor deadness. On the contrary, it is an experience full of life. Neither is it a fake oneness. It is not a merging with all that is around so that no responsibility exists for what is going on. Nor is it a blotting out or losing the boundaries of self. It is presence meeting Presence with all of the vitality of such an encounter.

Even those who are not in this triad will recognize what is described here as something they know at times. Nevertheless, this is the reality most consonant with 8/9/1 individuals and natural to how they are incarnated in this world. They turn to this approach frequently and find it is what best makes them pray-ers.

Approaches to the
Interior Life
for the 2/3/4 Triad

Formal prayer times are usually spent just quieting down for 2/3/4s, just stopping all the movement and activity, all the energy expended in the outer world. This is the doing triad. People in this part of the Enneagram often look emotional, but they are often so taken with action that they are out of touch with their feelings. It is important to remember that inner experience is dependent on emotion or affect. Inner experience actually becomes so and energizes precisely because it is emotional and affective. And it is the emotional, affective area that is least accessible to people in this triad. Often they will imitate the emotion present in the surrounding environment, but the actual experience of feeling is hard for them to touch into. Their instinctive turning to action and doing cuts off the life of the emotions within them.

Because of this dynamic, the task in life for 2/3/4s is to tend to themselves, to allow themselves the time and the quiet to actually experience their affective life and the energy that results from it. Tending themselves may also be termed "fanning their spirit," blowing on the cool coals of feeling that are within them. This will bring them to the warmth of love, of fear, of anger. In this fanning of their interior life of spirit they touch into the limitless Spirit. For this triad, the Spirit of Jesus alive in the world today has great significance. For all of us, of course, the Spirit of Jesus has meaning, but for 2/3/4s it is this aspect of the Divine that symbolizes their natural, spiritual way.

Emotion testifies to a life within, to an interior life. People in the 2/3/4 space usually are eager for emotion. They do not fear being overwhelmed by emotion the way 8/9/1 people do. A man in the 8/9/1 triad once told me about a recurring dream in which he stood on the seashore and was submerged by waves that came ashore and dragged him into their undertow. For him, those waves symbolized the drowning that so much feeling caused him. 2/3/4s, on the other hand, are eager for feelings because they know the vitality such experiences bring them. The dry dullness and emptiness of mere activity vanishes when emotion, whether pleasant or unpleasant, takes over. If there is any fear for 2/3/4s, it is that the emotions will be so many and so strong that they will not be able to function efficiently any longer. To function efficiently is, after all, what constitutes their value; they define themselves by what they do.

People in this triad need to learn to let emotions "take them." Instead of "having anger" they need to "be angry." They need to seethe and rage rather than merely tell themselves they are angry, as though observing the feeling from outside and putting a label on it. It is better for them to let their anger be their prayer than to pray about their anger. The straightforward experience of anger is the prayer, not the organizing and naming that they "have anger." Jesuit priest and spiritual leader Anthony deMello touches very well into this need of the 2/3/4s in his books.[2] He is probably in this triad himself. He talks about no longer standing as an evaluator of one's experience and analyzing it, but rather living it. Self-evaluation is a problem in the 2/3/4 space. Self-observation is an activity, a doing of something; it critiques and measures experience from the outside.

The spirituality of this triad is a horizontal one. God is not above for 2/3/4s but within themselves and others. When they can touch this spirit within themselves—which means when they can let their emotions have their own life—they find, as Karlfried von Durckheim has said, in that very same act, More than Themselves.[3] To the degree that one is present with the self, one is also present to the Greater Than Self. It is through this allowing their emotions to live that 2/3/4s find the Presence we have described in the 8/9/1 triad. Since 2/3/4s are so aware of the spirit that lives in themselves and in others, they instinctively look for God in human beings. This is where their personal "incarnate divinity" and that of others meets The Divine who is the Source of Life. They meet God when they look deeply into their own hearts and the hearts of other people.

What constitutes quietism, that menace to the life of prayer in all of the triads, in this one? To say it another way, what is avoidance of spirituality like in this triad? Very frequently, what 2/3/4s tend to call "centering" is really quietism. Active at all costs, they will often proceed to "making their interior mental screen blank," and call it centering. It is as though they shut off the jets of their energy with the result that they are bored and sleepy rather than alive and vital. David Steindl-Rast in his book *Gratefulness, the Heart of Prayer*, talks about a spider that simply does what it does.[4] *Age quod agis*—Do what you are doing—is what the old spiritual masters advised seekers. The spider simply makes his web. If someone comes along and destroys this web, the spider does not become agitated or upset. It continues in the next succession of moments to create another web.

There is a difference between watching an hour in prayer and watching for the duration of an hour. To watch for the duration of the hour usually leads to quietism; it is to stand by until sixty minutes have passed. To watch the hour is to be present to all that is happening in that hour, moment to moment. One time, when I was very upset and angry at something that had happened at the breakfast table, I found myself distracted during the prayer hour that followed. I tried to "blank my screen" and calm myself in order to concentrate on the Scripture passage I had chosen for reflection. In desperation, I finally decided to let my mental efforts go and to just be the angry person I was at that moment. The time passed quickly after that, and I was alert and focused. When I picked up the Scripture passage at the end of the hour it spoke with a clarity and relevance I had missed the first time around when I was trying to suppress the very feelings the passage addressed. That is the kind of interiority 2/3/4s need to have, rather than a calm, cool, emotionless, and detached state.

A quiet, complacent attitude where one is thinking nothing is to have an idol. Nothing is really "No Thing," which is, as Thomas Merton has said, "Some Thing."[5] In the quietism of this space, the worship of a blank No Thing is idolatry. Merton calls it the worship of a purely finite being absorbed in itself and its own triviality. Sam Keen says that, when we become preoccupied with our own egos and our own image of who we are, we become narcissistic navel-gazers.[6] But when we address the genuine reality of ourselves as we truly are, both the things we like and don't like about what we see, we are no longer narcissistic. We are, instead, in the painful and confronting process of conversion or transformation. When, on the other hand, our purpose is to enter into darkness, we have made a god of this darkness. Our purpose needs to be to enter into God just as we are at any given moment.

Approaches to the Interior Life for the 5/6/7 Triad

How does the 5/6/7 triad approach the interior life? How do these people find that pray-er who lives within? Their task is to honor their own experience and value it as worthwhile. This triad is where the Word of God, Jesus, God's Son, joins with their own individual word. They need to look to their own incarnation, to their own enfleshed experience. Little by little, they need to let their personal human reality open up to themselves, first of all, and then to other people. They need to involve their senses in whatever is going on. They, the highly perceptive individuals, need to avoid overusing that visual sense, by which they stand aside and look. They also need to touch, to taste, to smell. In addition, they need to pay attention to their kinesthetic sense, that internal experience that will reveal their centeredness or lack of centeredness, their "on" or "offness," if you will. Doing so will tell them when they are dry and fleshless and functioning completely from their heads. They need to beware of a shallow, withered, interior life that stops the free movement from inside to outside. They need to find an outlet for their energy, a flow that will prevent their becoming detached from their own life and the life around them. In other words, people in this triad need to watch lest they become tangled in perceptions and insights rather than penetrating beneath them to their physical and emotional response to their mental activity.

People in the 5/6/7 spaces tend to be very literal. They stick to what they see, to the facts, to data. Because of this, they are often blind to levels other than the merely perceptual. They look for some "key," a central connecting truth that will make everything fall into place and make sense. They need to learn that there is no such thing as a "key," and this is a concept often frightening to 5/6/7s who need to have an interior system that adds up, brings order, and gives them a feeling of safety. In working with a woman who was very enthusiastic about the Enneagram, I was describing how helpful she might find it on her spiritual journey. She responded, "Yes, it gives me a key to everything; the Enneagram is the key." I reminded her that there is no ultimate key, and I saw terror in her eyes at the very thought that she might never find what she considered so essential.

In the 5/6/7 spaces, rather than find some answer that will unlock all reality, it is necessary to come to the awareness that the process of living is the only solution. The unfolding, ongoing meaning of life, living it day by day, is what is called for. As we move step by step in the spiritual life, which I would also call the genuine human life, we discover its meaning by living it.

The prayer that is very natural and important for this triad is a dialogic kind of prayer, a conversation with the Divine. Jesus is the inspiration for the lives of people in this triad. Of course Jesus is the inspiration for us all, but Jesus is especially significant in this regard for 5/6/7s. Jesus himself introduced us to a dialogic prayer when he gave us the Our Father and told us, when asked how one should pray, that this was the way to do so.

The importance of dialogic prayer in the 5/6/7 triad is that it leads these persons from an excessive focus on the interior, a passive drinking in of experience, sucking in of the environment, to expansion and giving out. It involves saying who one is and what one believes and how one loves. It includes telling how one responds to the Divine. Thus, this dialogic prayer brings the 5/6/7 person out of isolation and into relationship with the Other. 8/9/1s struggle back and forth, finding life blocked off into segments: interior/exterior, spirit/flesh, self/God. It is their simple prayer of being that removes those boundaries and divisions so that balance means holding all of reality without boundaries, without shifting from one to the other. For the 5/6/7s, it is moving out that leads to a balance. Excessive holding in of energy is moderated by a giving out in the dialogue of prayer.

Simply breathing can become an important symbol in this triad. Opening out is what needs to be learned, rather than collecting concepts and trying to fit them into an interior system. All of us need to watch for quietism, of course. Quietism is the opposite of contemplation. It is not looking with eyes open at life, but rather avoiding looking straight at reality. The quietism of the 5/6/7 triad often takes the form of pure head work, hyperperceiving, that compulsive living in the mind. This head work leads to an unhealthy detachment from the reality of self, of other people, and of God, and consequently from the reality of the spiritual life.

The interior approach of the 2/3/4 triad revolves around what they often speak of as a "problem" with the interior life. These are the people who in compulsion move to the outer world. They search for connections among people, for binding among people. This is not the binding of affective, emotional linking that really brings people into one another's presence, but the more external connecting that organizes the outer world. The way 5/6/7s organize their interior lives, 2/3/4s tend to organize their external lives and relationships among people. Their life is very much spent outside themselves when they are in compulsion. When they find balance and centeredness, 2/3/4s move within.

In summary, then, 8/ 9/1s need to step back from an either/or stance to a both/and one, seeing and holding the whole continuum of reality. 5/6/7s come to center by adding an outer emphasis to their instinctive inner one. 2/3/4s need to find center and balance with an interior life that gives depth to their instinctual outer emphasis.

METHODS IN THE
LIFE OF PRAYER

Focusing as a Way to
Nourish the Interior
Life

Here we are considering focusing in the formal sense as it has been developed by Eugene Gendlin, whose book, *Focusing,* discusses this method.[1] Very briefly, he describes focusing as getting in touch with the "felt sense" of our experience, the effect of our experience on our total person: mind, body, feelings. He talks about the fact that everyone who is self-reflective focuses. Why do some people change and mature and others do not? Gendlin tells us that those who grow in insight and awareness are the ones who have learned to pay attention to what their entire persons are saying to them.

What Gendlin has done is provide a way for people to take into account not only their thoughts and feelings about something, but their bodily sense around it. Rather than leave these understandings to chance, he has developed several steps to make conscious that bodily sense, and he teaches how to "read" the insights and decisions our organism knows and "tells us" about our responses to circumstances in our lives. He describes the "Aha," that we know as "That's what this is about" or "That's what this means" and which we feel throughout our whole persons. He provides a method to "click into" that organismic knowing that gives us certainty and conviction and the assurance we need to embrace our truths and make necessary life changes. To put it another way, his method assists us in discerning what we are called to along our spiritual Way.

Gendlin has separated six different steps in this process. I won't go into these, but I would like to talk about the different ways people in the Enneagram triads approach the focusing methods he outlines and which of the steps are especially significant for each.

The 8/9/1 Triad

Very important in the 8/9/1 triad, where people can become drowned by their emotions, is to disidentify from their experience. They need to actually separate from the often overwhelming waves of their affective responses. Gendlin's first steps in the focusing method direct people to put outside themselves in imagination the subject of their focusing and look at it.

Keeping this distance helps 8/9/1s gain perspective and lessens the fear of their being washed away by their emotions around whatever it is they are considering. When they do gain this distance and perspective, the terror of being overwhelmed is lessened, and they are able to clarify, to differentiate, to synthesize, to objectify what they are focusing on. What the initial focusing steps do for this triad is help them see that being present to what is going on will not wipe them out, will not be too much for them to address. Instead, it will say to them that they are more than this consideration and that they can objectively address and master it. Also, when they do achieve some interior distance, they come to see how this current experience interrelates with other experiences. 8/9/1s need to find this detachment in order to look at something that would otherwise be too frightening or overwhelming to attend to. Then they can ask the next questions with confidence: What is this about for me? What does it mean for me?

The 5/6/7 Triad

5/6/7s need to get away from that detached kind of observing from outside. This triad needs to touch into the emotion of an experience. They need to be reminded that they have an organism that is the channel of their feelings. They have a body through which their feelings are expressed. They need to respect and pay attention to more than their ideas and perceptions and to their feeling and bodily functions as well. When they include in their awareness their emotions and the resonance of these in their bodies, they can be drawn into the "felt sense." The focusing step that inquires of the body what is going on leads them to their emotions and helps them include the wider gamut of data their entire organism is presenting to them. Unlike the 8/9/1 triad, they do not fear what might happen were they to touch into their emotional life. Like the 2/3/4 triad, they welcome the information their emotions provide.

The 2/3/4 Triad

For 2/3/4s it is important to take inside one's self whatever is the subject of one's focusing, be it a situation, a relationship, a problem, a question. This triad needs to "swallow" what is going on in the present. They need in their imagination to encircle it or, in another image, to take it into their mouths and let it slip down into their gut. The focusing step that encourages doing so is the most significant one for them. After they have embraced their experience they then need to wait for what happens rather than dictate a response, rather than "do something" about it. They need to patiently allow what feelings are present, which is to say where their energy lies. They need to experience Gendlin's "felt sense" through their body, their primary avenue to emotion or feeling, since they are such body/behavior/doing people. Perhaps Eugene Gendlin is in this triad and that is why he makes the body the channel for finding the "felt sense." For whatever reason he has come to emphasize the bodily function, this method has been a significant contribution to self-awareness, especially for people who are out of touch with their feelings.

In summary, then, it is more profitable for 5/6/7s and 2/3/4s in some way to imagine that they take in and surround the experience they are looking to uncover for themselves. It is important, on the other hand, for 8/9/1s not to swallow what they are focusing on, not to take it in. They are already overwhelmed with emotion and do not need to emphasize it. Rather, they need to put whatever it is they are attending to outside themselves in order to gain the distance that will give them perspective and mastery.

IMAGE AND SYMBOL AS
A WAY TO NOURISH THE
INTERIOR LIFE

I would like to extend this discussion of becoming more and more aware of one's reality beyond the focusing technique of Eugene Gendlin's to a broader consideration of images and symbols and their message for our lives.

The 8/9/1 Triad

8/9/1 people tend to think analogically. They tend to use analogies: "This is like something else." They speak in imagery even more than other triads. For example: "I just got run over by a ten-ton truck."

or "I feel like I could take off and fly." Even though this analogical and metaphorical speaking is true for them and even though they use a great deal of simile, they often dismiss their images and symbols as unimportant. Often they do not notice this avenue to understanding themselves. They may be unaware they are using images and symbols or, if they do see what they are doing, they often dismiss what this tendency offers them in self-understanding. To pay attention to their images and symbols is to find perceptive insight and the perspective 8/9/1s on their spiritual journey are looking for.

Just what do these images and symbols provide for 8/9/1s? The massive feelings that seemed overwhelming and disconnected can cluster around a concrete focus, around something specific. They often feel that there is too much going on for mere words, that they cannot get their minds around their experience. When they do attend to their images and symbols, the perceptive function which often evades them comes into use. While their imagery is often visual, it can also be auditory, kinesthetic, gustatory, or tactile. Something is perceived and around that specific sense perception their emotion then clusters. This emotion, so amorphous and immense when free-flowing, now has parameters. Connections are made around this image which then involves the activity function. Questions are asked of it and insights occur. The image is "worked with" in various ways.

The constant inner/outer struggle of this triad, with their sliding back and forth and attending to one aspect and excluding the other, is quieted. The image involves some thing which gathers and involves the whole person. Said another way, the inner experience and outer reality come together into one response. Thus the division of inner/outer is cut through and the searching struggle to find their genuine experience grows less. The meaning and emotion are captured in a single image or symbol. There is no need for rational, dry thinking with feelings squashed and wiped out, something 8/9/1s are sometimes tempted to call the interior or spiritual life. For every triad, the interior and spiritual life will of necessity be affective/emotional because life means energy. Without emotion, as the bioenergeticists have taught us, there is no energy. There is a processing that goes on in working with images and symbols for this triad, but it is a non-cognitive kind of processing. It is not only mental, head activity, nor just emotional, heart activity, nor instinctive, gut activity. It is a response of the whole person, of the entire organism. The 8/9/1 triad needs to learn and become comfortable with the fact that their knowing will always come through the channel of their affections.

There are certain common images and symbols I have found 8/9/1s turning to because of their outlook on life and their own particular needs and issues. One of these images is that of a sailboat controlled by a rudder. People in this space who fear getting blown away by emotions often need to remind themselves that they are in command of the vessel of themselves, symbolized by their hand on the rudder. Depending on how they manage that rudder they either are aligned with the wind or are bucking it. Their issue around emotional energy is seen as a call to flow with rather than struggle against their life flow.

Another image that 8/9/1s speak of as helpful is that of standing on the shoreline of a body of water and experiencing the waves coming in, but only up to their toes. They are not pulled under or drowned by these waves, even though the tide comes ever closer. When it does so, they have the power to step back as the waves approach. Again, this insight reminds them that they are in control and not victims of their strong emotions. When their affections become frighteningly strong and encroaching, they can choose to move away and not be drowned. It is, indeed, important for people in this triad to experience self-mastery. They need to feel powerful rather than the victims of undisciplined feelings which erase the possibility of conscious attention to their life's issues.

The 5/6/7 Triad

Image and symbol provide a different service for 5/6/7s. In this triad there is a need to be pulled out from their interior place so that the inner and outer aspects of their reality can be balanced and they can be more centered. Whatever image or symbol does pull them out is valuable for them. Sometimes music is helpful, especially when performed by themselves, such as singing or playing an instrument. This involves their activity function and also captures the emotions. In working with a guitarist who was having a dry, lifeless retreat, I suggested she use some songs rather than Scripture passages to pray with. She sang and played, and her retreat began to open up as she touched feelings and expressed her inner affective perceptiveness. Perhaps in this triad more than in the others it is important to enter a prayer experience with eyes open. While this can be counterproductive for the other triads, for 5/6/7s it can prevent them from getting lost in the complexity of their thoughts and meanderings through their inner mazes. With eyes open they can focus on something concrete and exterior rather than pursue a myriad of thoughts. Some images and symbols that people in this triad have said were helpful as an outer focus are a burning candle, a crucifix, an icon, or a flower. Anything that says to them that they are part of the outer world can keep them from losing themselves down endless mental pathways.

Assuming various postures is also helpful in the 5/6/7 triad. This reminder that they are physical, incarnate, bodily, also reduces their mental overemphasis. In most cases, spontaneous and creative movement to music or to a suggested emotion is probably too much for them, at least at the beginning of their journeys.

Generally speaking, people in this triad are too self-conscious about their bodies to move into free expression. Having said this, the assumption of a posture and staying with it does involve the body without making it a constant preoccupation during the time of prayer.

Another symbol that is often helpful for 5/6/7s is that of physical nakedness. This seems true for a number of reasons. First of all, it says to them: "I have a body. When I have my clothes off, I am more aware of my body. I can feel the air on my body's surface. I see my reality uncovered." Also, nakedness symbolizes a desire to be known. It uncovers hiding and reveals the private person not only to self, but to God as well. It is a physical statement that indicates they want God to know them in their totality. This is a symbolic action similar to the words in Psalm 139 which speak to God about his all-knowing presence.[2] Nakedness is also a statement of openness and vulnerability. Clothes can be like armor; they protect from being known, from being obvious, from being wounded. When people remove their clothes they are unprotected and trusting.

Praying face down on the floor can be a powerful bodily symbol for 5/6/7s. Praying with hands open in their laps testifies to an attitude of openness and receptivity to being taken by God. In this space, the emotional function is not primary as it is in the 8/9/1 triad. Nevertheless it is the auxiliary or helping function and is therefore generally accessible to 5/6/7s.[3] By moving beyond perceptions into feelings this triad can be led into action, a part of reality they tend to neglect. It is the world of action they are being called to as they are drawn to expand their experiences and make their lives more whole.

Slow walking is also helpful in leading them from their interior into outer activity. It says what their spirituality calls them to. They need to let God lead them forth, step by step, on the journey. The spiritual life is a process. There is not, as we have said, a key that answers all, but a step-by-step living of each moment. Each of these moments possesses all that is sufficient. Every small step, slowly taken, tells them that they need not fear to be abandoned, unguarded, and alone, far from the safety of God's Providence. This is not the jogging that 8/9/1s often use to wake themselves up or 2/3/4s need to skim off the top level of their anxieties. It is the security found in venturing forth little by little into an often threatening world.

The 2/3/4 Triad

For the 2/3/4s the place of image and symbol has its particular nuance, as one might expect. People in this triad naturally find action and people leading them to the God within themselves. David Steindl-Rast in his book *Gratefulness, the Heart of Prayer* talks about the importance of being still and still moving.[4] I think for 2/3/4s, this reality is of particular significance. Because of the high level of anxiety in this triad, stillness is not a very frequent phenomenon. However, still moving can be. There is a quality of bodily activity that can symbolize the interior experience, so that when one is still and still moving one can be touching into the centered place of unity with the Divine.

Gracefulness, to be grace full, means to be full of gift which is what grace is. When one is full of gift and full of grace, one moves gracefully. This is a sign of interior centeredness for everyone. This being so, this graceful movement of their body may be the single sign, and sometimes the only sign, that can speak to 2/3/4s. For this reason, *hatha* yoga, which is the moving from one posture—or *asana*—to another, often speaks to their reality. For 2/3/4s it is the posture itself that is the symbol, the prayer. 8/9/1s frequently say that this form of yoga is for them a helpful prelude to prayer. 2/3/4s, on the other hand, are more inclined to say that hatha yoga is a helpful prayer. Distinguishing between posture and movement and prayer is better forgotten for 2/3/4s. For them, it is simply assuming the posture that constitutes the prayer.

People in the 2/3/4 triad will often be involved in massage or creative movement or bioenergetic kinds of exercises. The importance of these three body approaches is that they lead them to their feelings. If they don't lead them to feelings they are not of significance in helping this triad come to greater awareness. Creative movements that turn into a performance are not a prayer activity for persons in this triad. However, creative movement that expresses their sadness or their joy—that is their sadness or joy stated in action—is prayer. Bioenergetics, where people are asked to express their emotions and to speak them, as it were, in body movement is another kind of experience that can be prayer for 2/3/4s. It is interesting to note how many 2/3/4s instinctively in the course of their lives and in the course of deepening their spirituality turn to body experiences, especially massage. It is not uncommon that, when persons are physically touched in the act of receiving a massage, they begin to weep. The physical touch of being cared for, of having their body affirmed, tended to, respected, actually moves them to self-respect and self-tending. The tears that flow as a consequence of this awareness are an honoring of their persons. One workshop that I held revealed that all the 2/3/4s present, a group of more than one hundred people, had at one time or another, turned to massage as a way of getting in touch with their spirituality and the movements of their interior. To say it another way, massage had helped them grow in their contemplative life.

Motion that relieves, that "creams off" the top level of anxiety, is also helpful in times of prayer for 2/3/4s. Work that does not involve their minds, such as routine house-cleaning or other maintenance tasks, can free them for self-presence. Walking while praying is also freeing. Driving the car can be an aid to prayer. In all of these activities the mind is freed to go where it needs to go. When 2/3/4s do non-involving work they are not effortfully pursuing prayer, not trying to pray. Therefore, the interior world can become available and surprise them. Frequently, when 2/3/4s are not intending to pray, they pray much better.

It is often necessary for 2/3/4s to get away from their usual place of living and working, from the people and responsibilities and expectations in their environment, to be able to turn to interior pursuits. Remember, these are the people who are constantly asking "How am I doing?" If anyone is around where the assessment of how they are doing might happen, they will be distracted from simple presence to their reality, from contemplation. Philosopher Sam Keen, who I suspect is in this triad, has built a hermitage on the grounds of his own house where he spends a period of time·on a regular basis.[5] And, of course, there is Thomas Merton, whose longing for a hermit life was a theme and quest of his entire life.[6] This triad also finds it difficult to pray when others are nearby, even if not in their presence. As long as 2/3/4s are aware that people are somewhere around, there is a subtle interaction.

One of the best ways for 2/3/4s to find spiritual nourishment is for them to indulge in leisure when it is defined as doing what one feels like doing. What happens when people simply do what they feel like doing? First of all, they take into account themselves and their inner awarenesses. They inquire of themselves what is going on with them, something they often forget to do in this triad, so focused are they on the external world and peoples' issues. They opt for themselves as valuable rather than just people to be given away in doing for the concerns and desires of others. Also, when they ask "What do I feel like doing?" they are inquiring where their own energy is and, indirectly, what emotions they are experiencing. This is an activity that is necessary to come to presence with self. The result, therefore, is communion with self/Self, their own and the Divine Life that dwells within them. There they find God, and from there they can move to finding God in other people and the environment. They move from a situation in which their efforts are spent connecting with people to a presence which is a communion and genuine bonding with others. It is probably true that 2/3/4s need less time alone than people in the other triads. They actually move rather quickly from the inner to the outer life. While this is sometimes compulsive, it is also a natural phenomenon in this triad. It is through the spirit/Spirit alive in other people, once they are centered, that they are able to seek and find.

NATURE AND CREATION
AS A WAY TO NOURISH
THE INTERIOR LIFE

Surely, nature has an effect on all people. However, the different triads experience nature differently.

The 8/9/1 Triad

For 8/9/1s, the statement that nature makes often has something to do with their need for perspective. A woman I know in this triad loves the poster that shows a picture of our galaxy with a little dot, representing the earth, and an arrow pointing to it that says "You are here." This attitude toward creation is an important one for her. She sees herself, her particular existence, and this particular moment of it, in the perspective of the whole. Nature is all one. It does not fight against itself, but rather, has a pattern that it fulfills. This pattern contains more than an individual life. 8/9/1s need to see their personal, individual pattern as it plays into the greater pattern of the flow of creation.

Because of this attitude of perspective, there is also the possibility of holding everything at once rather than shifting back and forth between inner and outer, secular and sacred, and the other opposites as is the 8/9/1 tendency. Stepping back so that all can be held at once, all can be seen in one panoramic vision, is a reminder that God the Creator is the presence that holds the entire universe in existence, including one's self. This reality can lead 8/9/1s to centeredness.

Also in this space, which is so heavily moral, nature provides a statement that there is no need to judge. There is no morality in nature; nature simply is and in its existence is good.

The 5/6/7 Triad

For the 5/6/7 person nature speaks to a different kind of need. Nature tends to draw out people in this triad, to pull them into a world beyond their own interior one of perceptions. It is important for 5/6/7s to not merely glance at and nibble the reality outside, but to actually feast on its textures, colors, sounds, and tastes. This triad needs to look at things in nature, touch them, smell them, even taste them. They need to interact with nature as a member and part of nature. A particular aspect of nature that often appeals to 5/6/7s is the expanse of it. Nature is ordered and planned, testifying to a providential Creator. The vastness of sea, sky, and mountain vistas offers consolation. While they may make a person feel small, they also make one feel safe in an ordered whole that does not overpower and where limits and boundaries are present. Things are in their fitting and right place. Everything has such a place in the world, and there is a Limitless One who designs this.

The 2/3/4 Triad

For 2/3/4s another aspect of nature is seen as important. There is no demand in nature to interrelate as there is in the world of people. One need not go out to or take care of or connect with. No cloud needs to relate to another cloud, nor does one need to do more than observe the phenomenon the clouds present. There are no expectations and demands from nature. Nature simply is, and, instead of drawing them out to it, it leads them inward to self and feelings. A daily walk, for example, might best be done where there will not be people to meet along the way and where the route will not prove distracting. Even animals or some kind of perceived need in nature can lead 2/3/4s away from a freedom from expectations. A woman in this triad was walking a track one day when she spotted a squirrel struggling to carry off a large piece of bread. This squirrel in distress so captured her need to give care that she found it impossible to stay with her reflections. Normally, what nature does provide for 2/3/4s is a quiet space that allows them to look within themselves.

REMEMBERING AS A
WAY TO NOURISH THE
INTERIOR LIFE

An important aspect of the spiritual journey is the weaving for ourselves the story of our own lives. It is important to go back to our personal history and pay attention to it. Therefore memory and the way we remember and the things we remember and what memory provides us in our conversion are essential ingredients of spiritual growth.

The 8/9/1 Triad

8/9/1 persons carry along much unprocessed emotional life from the past. These people get stuck in the experiences of their history. They forget about their strong emotions from the past because of their frightening intensity. Having put them aside, they carry these feelings along unlived, unresolved, undigested into their present experiences. When they begin to remember their lives, they discover the child they were who lived back there in the past. That child is an innocent child, a vulnerable and excited, alive and eager child very different from the armored and self-protected adult they have become. The vulnerability turned to cynicism, boredom, and lifelessness as the years have passed.

The topic of remembering ties in with that of journaling, because journaling is where people tell themselves their story; where they write their own autobiographies. When they journal, 8/9/1s express their inner reality. They move from inside to outside. In the moments of their journaling, they hold the inner and outer together. Again we find a theme that is important in this triad. 8/9/1s live in a series of disconnected moments, of a succession of nows that have little or no connection with previous ones. They need, therefore, to do a literal connecting, factual remembering of what went on with them as long ago as their childhood and as close as yesterday. It is good for them to write down in their journals the "what," the facts of their experience from day to day. This serves as a reminder of what actually happened to them. Going back over these factual accounts, they can often discover why it is they feel as they do at this given moment. They have reviewed the experiences that led up to this moment and can understand it more fully. If they feel angry or resentful in the present, for example, it is often helpful for them to go back over events to see how often they may have experienced frustrating situations like the present one and come to awareness as to why they are reacting so strongly now. Without that kind of literal remembering, 8/9/1s are often unclear as to why the emotions they have now are present. These strong responses seem to have no reason or explanation.

Pictures and other graphics are important for 8/9/1s. This fact relates to what has been mentioned concerning images and symbols and their way of clustering emotions and giving them focus. Therefore, a journal composed of pictures and graphics can be helpful to remembering in this triad, because they capture more than words can. A man I knew from this triad told me that he never wrote words in his journal. To adequately describe his experience to himself would take him fifty pages of text, something he had neither time nor interest in writing. Instead, he would draw a picture where each line had a meaning, where the colors chosen said something. The medium and the texture this medium made possible said something about what he was feeling, as did, of course, the content.

I had occasion to work with a woman in this triad who found it impossible to articulate her affective experience. I suggested to her that at the end of every day she sit down before a piece of paper, pick up any colors from the box in front of her, and begin to draw without any particular intention. At first she saw no meaning in this process nor in the drawings that resulted; she simply did what was suggested. However, as time went on, she began to notice more in the shapes she was drawing, in the way those developed over time, and the changes in colors she chose and how these colors blended with others. She became aware that in this sequence, themes were emerging. She gradually found words for her experience: "I feel like I'm moving to a place of hope now. The green and yellow colors say that to me. I'm coming out of darkness." or "These heavy shapes are lighter and they don't seem as burdensome as they once were." Using these pictures as a base for our conversation, she was able to become very articulate about her emotional experiences and her interior reality.

The 5/6/7 Triad

Those in the 5/6/7 triad tend to neglect their history. They see others as considering them unimportant and of little account, and this is a projection of how they feel about themselves. While they do value their ideas, they see their own story as of little value, and they neglect it as well. It is therefore important for this triad to tell themselves the story of their lives. Probably in this space more than in any other the actual writing of an historical biography is helpful. Not only do they need to record the factual events, the circumstances, the people who have moved in and out of their lives, they also need to capture emotions. Again, affect is their auxiliary or helpful function. They need to get in touch with this part of themselves to have a felt sense of their history. In that way they re-member rather than merely recall. If you look at the word "remember," it means a putting back, reattaching disconnected members, parts of ourselves. When we simply "recall," we call memories out and run them past us again. In remembering, we put them back on to ourselves and meld them onto the whole of our lives. That is what adding emotion to mere recounting offers us.

It is important for 5/6/7s to go back and rejoice in the victories in their lives, the celebrations of their history. It is valuable as well for them to grieve their sadnesses, deaths, and losses. When they do that they find again the frightened child looking for safety, looking to be known, looking to be protected. Journaling in the 5/6/7 triad is a way of honoring their experience and a looking at not only what is finished, but also at what is unfinished, at what is ongoing. As the poet Rainer Maria Rilke has said, they need to be patient with what is unsolved in their heart, knowing that the process of life goes on day by day and step by step, never to be pieced together completely in their heads.[7]

The 2/3/4 Triad

For 2/3/4s the place of memory has a different emphasis. This triad tends to color its past nostalgically. They think about all the wonderful, romantic, fine, or pleasant experiences that happened back in the good old days; or, if it serves their life story better, they remember the bad, oppressive, and victimizing things that happened to them in the bad old days. For 2/3/4s, both tendencies to color the past provide either a positive or negative exaggeration of their real experiences. For them, returning in memory to the past becomes something of a work of fiction. Since 2/3/4s have such a hard time staying in the present moment, probably the best way for them to approach memory work is to do so from the present. They need to stay here, now, noticing what they are feeling in their body; and, consequently, through the body they become in touch with the feelings of any particular moment. From this awareness they can move to reflect on when in their life story they have felt this way before. What does this present awareness remind them of in their past? In this way they will come to know their child, often the anxious child trying to adapt or please or be accepted and so reduce conflict around them in the environment.

An example of this dynamic is that of a woman on the staff of a spirituality program who was working with two highly intellectual colleagues and engaged with them in a theology discussion. As they talked, she felt herself withdrawing and becoming increasingly discouraged and depressed. When she left their presence she told herself that she would have to leave her position because she was not intelligent and educated enough to be on par with the others she was working with. As she was driving home she remembered herself as a little girl, by far the youngest in her family. She recalled attempting to carry on a conversation with her oldest brother and sister, at the time young adults, about their lives and their world. As she spoke with them she saw an amused glance and a smile pass between them and realized that her comments had not only been inappropriate but irrelevant and humorous. She was not one of them, no matter how much she wanted to be; she was just a little girl. She immediately felt embarrassed and ran away. Then she remembered her recent conversation with her colleagues at work. She recalled that, while they were talking together, she seemed to be looking up at them as if she were a child looking at two adults. The following day when she was next in her colleagues' presence, she could honor and respect that little girl's experience, but realize she was now an adult herself, and a woman capable of addressing spiritual issues in a mature and informed, if somewhat different, way from that of her colleagues; she was now also grown-up and could look at them face to face. If she had not allowed that little girl into her memory with her feelings of embarrassment and separateness, she would not have understood the previous day's extreme feelings of diminishment and the

57

desire to flee. It was the memory and affect around her childhood experience that touched her into those same feelings in the present.

Journaling in the 2/3/4 triad includes what earlier spiritual writers used to call "composition of place." Oftentimes, when they pick up the pen and book used for journaling 2/3/4s find presence to themselves. This is probably also true for persons in the other triads, but it seems especially true for 2/3/4s who often can only touch their emotions when they journal. This triad needs also to beware of a neat and organized journal with lovely pictures and good handwriting. The journal for people in this triad, if they are to touch into their feelings, including their most buried feeling which is anger, will probably look messy.

If it is a good journal it will be unappraised and possibly written either on loose leaf paper or in a spiral notebook so that they can tear out pages and throw them away. The more embarrassing and emotional passages can be easily and immediately disposed of. It is not important for 2/3/4s to look back at what they have written. They have, after all, a panoramic view of past, present, and future and rarely become stuck in the present. It is not important for them to keep what they have written for continuity. It is more important to be in an experience here and now. The journal that is uncensored, unconcerned as to what people might think, can provide that freedom. It can offer an opportunity to jot down, even gouge out with their pen part of the pages as they write of their anger, resentment, fear, sadness, frustration, and ecstasy. Afterward, these pages can be destroyed.

WORKING WITH DREAMS
AS A WAY TO NOURISH
THE INTERIOR LIFE

Many people testify to the importance of dream work in their spiritual development. One reason for this interest is that the images and symbols in our dreams are not of our choice; instead, they choose us. They come to us from our unconscious life and so are not only specific to us, but more free from our control.

I have a dream theory that applies to the Ennea-gram. It is one I use when paying attention to my own dream life and in companioning others in their dream work. It is based on the recognized dream theory that what we dream about is what we are not aware of when we are awake. While our conscious life is in our awareness, the spiritual journey invites us to know more and more of our reality beyond the tip of the iceberg that is our consciousness. This unconscious of ours uses, among other means, what we dream of when we are asleep in order to reveal more of what we miss when awake.

An image I have of a dream is that of a photographic negative of our conscious life. The things we are conscious of when we are awake, the bright areas in the printed photograph of our awake lives, are what are dark in our asleep life. We do not need to look at them as much because we are already doing so. It follows that the dark areas of the printed photograph of our conscious lives are what show up bright on the negative, that is, in the dream. These are the areas we need to learn more about so that we can expand our conscious awareness of ourselves and our journey. It would follow that what we are least aware of in our Enneagram triad would be what would be highlighted in our dream life. What we attend to least of all when awake would be what we need to attend to in our asleep dreams. To say it another way, what is in the darkness of our conscious awareness is what will shine when we sleep; the bright areas of our dreams are what we need to pay attention to; they offer new information for our growth. Now I will apply this theory to the different triads.

The 8/9/1 Triad

For the 8/9/1 triad, it is the perceptual function that is least accessible and so least instinctively known. This perceptual function makes connections between one concept and another, one awareness and another. Therefore, it is those connections, those aspects of the imagery in the dream, that 8/9/1s need to attend to most of all. The founders of gestalt therapy were probably in this triad. The techniques they have developed for working with dreams have to do with associations, deepened perceptions, and relationships between discrete parts of the dream. It is the focus on perceptual interconnectedness that underlies their approach to dream work. This is not the place to go deeply into gestalt methods.[8] I will simply say that the gestalt way of doing dream work seems to enlighten 8/9/1s more than other techniques. Having written the dream story in the present tense, the dreamer considers the different parts of the narration one by one and associates around them. This can be done by identifying with each image, associating around it and, as it were, becoming it, and finally speaking as it. This helps the dreamer to touch into the way different parts of the dream interact and interrelate.

For example, if I have a dream where I pick up a knife and peel an apple, it might be helpful to identify with the apple, to become it and speak as it, and let it speak to the knife. I can then identify with the knife and follow the same procedure. What happens in this approach, which is part of the gestalt methodology, is that the relationships with the different parts of the dream, the various images and symbols in the dream, begin to connect. I begin to see more and more of the relationships between aspects of the dream until I become aware of the whole picture, the design that brings the aspects together.

The 5/6/7 Triad

For the 5/6/7 triad it is the behavioral or activity function that is least accessible. This is the darkest part of their awareness when they are awake and therefore, is what the unconscious would be likely to highlight when they are asleep. The actions and points of decision in the dream, including whether or not decisions were made, are areas to be attended to in this triad's dream work. "Did I or did I not do something in this dream? What did I do? How did I choose? What was my behavior? What was the progression of my actions?" These are helpful 5/6/7 questions. At least initially, looking at the dream story itself can prove enlightening. The beginning, the middle, the turning point, the end of a dream should be the focus. To consider all of the movement, all of the process the dream and the dreamer go through, is often helpful in this triad.

Author and Jungian analyst Robert A. Johnson, who has some good advice about dream work, talks about actually doing something about the dream in one's awake life. He speaks about one of his own dreams that took place in a certain residential city block.[9] After he worked with the dream he actually went to that spot and walked around the block. This method touches into the 5/6/7 bodily or activity function and actually serves to draw the dreamer out from the interior world into concretely doing something about the dream. I do not think that such grounding, as it is called, is necessary for the other triads, especially for 2/3/4s. It would be better for 2/3/4s to stay with the emotions of the dream than to get up and do something about it and so risk getting caught into their doing compulsion.

The 2/3/4 Triad

Moving on to what is helpful for 2/3/4s, we find their buried function to be the affective function. For this reason, to recount the activity of the dream might not be all that important for them. It would seem that what would be most useful is to pay attention to feelings and emotions. While it may be well to sketch out the story sequence in the dream just to retain it in memory, it is best to follow that step by going back over the events and paying attention to the feelings that arise around them, and whether these change through the course of the narration. It is good for this triad to concentrate on the story of the emotions rather than the story of the events in the dream. This results in a feeling summary of the dream in present tense. For example, besides summarizing the content of a dream about being in prison, a 2/3/4 might address the feelings that this evokes: "I feel like I am imprisoned, frustrated, held in, frightened, although I know that somehow and someday I will be liberated from this place."

It is also helpful, especially for 2/3/4s, to notice the feelings they have on waking up. Are they energized, depressed, discouraged, frightened, burdened, anxious, irritated? Whatever the feeling might be on waking, that time can provide important clues concerning what the unconscious is trying to reveal, whether or not there are memories of the night's dreaming.

Prayer in Common as a Way to Nourish the Interior Life

Common prayer is an aspect of spiritual growth that almost all of us find ourselves involved in. We are, after all, social beings who do not live as separate islands. Most of us pray with other people, at least at times, and many participate regularly in some form of liturgical prayer. Common prayer with its effects on individual pray-ers is not often a topic for discussions about spirituality. Here I would like to share some thoughts on the value of common prayer for the different triads and what aspects of that prayer are most helpful for each. These are seed thoughts on a topic that has not been pursued in depth. We note here once again that the Enneagram is an ever-evolving theory, dependent upon people's shared experiences. Especially on this topic, which has not as yet been well developed, additional information gleaned from personal wisdom is needed to flesh out the following comments.

The 8/9/1 Triad

It seems that 8/9/1s often experience a boredom and burdensomeness during prayers in common. As a consequence, there sometimes is a resistance to attending common prayer gatherings. One reason for that, as some people in this triad report, is that image and symbol are rarely used or are superficially presented. Consequently, there is nothing to attract and stir their affect and draw them into the experience. Another reason for not liking common prayer is found in the opposite of this problem. This occurs when images and symbols are over-used, and 8/9/1 participants find themselves on an emotional roller coaster, pulled from feeling to feeling. A related issue is when the emotion proposed in the common prayer is dissonant with a current strong emotion of the 8/9/1 pray-er. One way 8/9/1s may respond to these issues in their common prayer life is aggression, both passive and active, depending on what their number is in the triad. It would seem that passive aggression is more common than active; to complain publicly about a prayer experience does not seem this triad's preferred response. Rather, not to comply with liturgical instructions about standing, sitting, or gesturing, not to keep the tempo of the group in word or song, seem the more likely way 8/9/1s make known their dissatisfaction with the prayer experience. The ultimate passivity is, of course, to remove one's presence completely from common prayer because it is judged unsatisfactory.

Sometimes 8/9/1s come with a cynical attitude to the ritual that has been planned. Even though that may be the way they come, they can sometimes be "grabbed" by the symbol and taken up into the prayer. Such a response is similar to the way this triad responds to imagery and symbolism generally. They may not pay attention to this analogical aspect of themselves. They may overlook or see as unimportant the images and symbols that are theirs. Yet, having said that, they are often taken into profound experiences through this avenue when they are caught unawares.

People in this triad often say that having a single theme in common prayer helps them. Something where the song, the readings, and the actions all express the same kind of energy touches them to their feelings. When caught by this energy, it is easier for them to stay with it to a consistent, focused prayer time. When caught up by the affective energy of the prayer, this triad loses the boundaries separating them from themselves and from the other pray-ers and beyond to the unity of creation; they open to genuine shared prayer and know one voice, one heart, and one mind.

It seems that prayer in common for 8/9/1s has a back and forth quality. Sometimes there is a commitment to prayer; at other times they choose not to show for a time. They often move from fidelity to indifference in this, as in other aspects of their lives. Sometimes, even when their words announce firm commitment, their behaviors demonstrate what is going on with the back and forth, the here and absent. There is the reaching out in loving attention that makes for fruitful prayer for 8/9/1s. From the hard work of being together, of rubbing against others, of being confined with a group during prayer time, nourishment can be drawn. These persons can move from struggle to opening and receiving the gift/grace of love and unity like rain from above.

The 5/6/7 Triad

For 5/6/7s with regard to common prayer we again see the issue of not being important or of much account. They think no one will miss them if they are not there. Their presence is unimportant. On the other hand, they often see it as a duty to attend to common prayer. If the rule or the law says that the group should gather, they see it as what needs to be done and their presence as what the authority or the person in charge expects of them. This can sometimes lead to a pharisaical keeping tabs on who are and who are not doing what they are supposed to do. They came and fulfilled their duty; where are the others and why are they missing? The issue of fidelity rather than duty is an important one in the 5/6/7 triad. It is important to be faithful to themselves and to other people rather than grimly and with set jaw to carry out orders. They are called in common prayer to a relationship of trust as regards others and God. The symbol of gathering together is a statement of this triad's mutual trust and their oneness in fidelity to the Divine.

Intercessory prayer is important for 5/6/7s. It moves them outside of their heads and helps them express themselves and to see and ask for and care about what they and others need. This is, once again, a dialogic kind of prayer. The place of prayer with its objects, rituals, clothing, and words reveals their inner lives. They speak out loud together; they learn to be with one another in the outer world, outside of that private place where they encounter God. The liturgical space with its symbols calls them forth to meet God among other people. They learn that they can meet God gathered together as well as by themselves.

Eucharist, another aspect of liturgy, eating the Body and Blood of the Divine, often has a special importance for 5/6/7 people. Jesus said, "Take and eat; this is my Body."[10] In this command, common prayer becomes more than relating to God as other. They are assimilated by God. In Eucharist, not only do they take in the Word of God, 5/6/7s become sharers in this Word when they and God are joined as one. This becomes an important distinction for 5/6/7s who are used to chewing on life, taking it in, swallowing it. In the Eucharist they not only take in, they are taken in, changed, and made new. The Divine completely absorbs them out of themselves and into union.

The 2/3/4 Triad

For 2/3/4 persons, the Body of Christ, alive and experienced here and now in this gathering is the important aspect of Eucharistic celebration. All are one in the Spirit of Christ Jesus and the Divine Spirit is alive here through all the individual spirits who are present. Common prayer for this triad is a gathering of God who is here and now because people are present here and now. In the presence of all, God is present. For 2/3/4s there is often little attention to what is taking place in the liturgical prayer itself. This can also be said of other forms of common prayer. This triad will often leave a place of gathering without reflections, thoughts, or movement in their hearts. Nevertheless, prayer in common is not mere ritual; it is a symbol. The gathering itself is what is important for them. What people do when they gather is not so important as the fact that they come together. When 2/3/4s are in a group of people gathered in prayer they are usually very aware of the individual persons there and experience support in the presence of the community. Often in a group of people, this triad is taken with concerns about those people and the quality of their relationships with them. Those gathered bring the Spirit of Jesus into this moment.

Another aspect of prayer in common that is important for 2/3/4s is that of the various roles that are part of the ritual. Who lights the fire? Who reads the Scripture passage? Who walks in the procession? Each person has a proper place in this communion of people. Each has a task, a function, a role, and this includes both themselves and other people in the group. The Body is made up of all together. There is one action, the action of giving and receiving, and it is important for 2/3/4s to listen to the word, to be ministered to, to be greeted. The back and forth of receiving and giving becomes the rhythm of their prayer in common and of liturgy. A rhythm that is too much their creation, their work, tends to get 2/3/4s into their compulsive activity function with its accompanying superficiality.

Very often, when 2/3/4s leave a liturgical experience or other common prayer, they will only remember who they saw there and what went on with those others. Nevertheless, the gathering testifies to and reminds them of the reality that spirit has both a large and a small "S." When they are truly with themselves in this common prayer experience they know they are united to that Divine Presence—Divine Spirit—that is within themselves and within others. The particular aspects of the prayer experience take on a secondary role, and the symbolic statement that all of us are united is the important message for this triad.

Eastern Prayer Forms as a Way to Nourish the Interior Life

Many people in the Western world who are looking to deepen their spiritual lives find help in Eastern prayer forms. Perhaps the reason for this attraction is that the Eastern forms are more wholistic. They take into account the total person, the entire human organism, the mind/feeling/body integrated and considered as one. One parallel to this approach in the West is focusing as developed by Eugene Gendlin which we have already discussed. His method is to invoke the body for the felt sense of a person's experience. There is no need to fear Eastern prayer forms if we consider them rightly. They offer helps for every human being and touch into universal ways for people to become pray-ers, whatever their cultural backgrounds. Human nature is the same the world over. People may name experiences differently, but the reality of growing to wholeness is the same for us all. Thomas Merton was one of the first in our time who understood this truth and helped us to recognize it.[11]

The 8/9/1 Triad

With this as a preface, let us look at the 8/9/1 approach to Eastern prayer forms in general and to which ones speak most to them. This triad often says that yoga is a helpful preparation for their prayer experience. One of the reasons why that may be the case is that the body is the helping or auxiliary function for 8/9/1s. This doing/behavioral function leads them to the perceptual connections that enlighten their experience. The kind of yoga mentioned here is hatha yoga, which consists of postures into which bodies are shaped. These postures, or asanas, often bring 8/9/1s to a place of centering. If, however, assuming these postures is seen as a secular activity, one not qualifying as something spiritual, 8/9/1s might prefer a modification of it by using their bodies to mime Scripture. Actually taking a posture suggested by the reading of a Bible passage or acting out a Scripture story can become helpful for them to develop their own, as it were, religious asanas. Secular and spiritual can then be brought together for them.

Also, in no other triad of the Enneagram is Zen more helpful. Zen involves presence in the here and now and flowing with whatever reality is in this moment. It includes being with whatever feeling, thought or sensation arises. One image to describe the Zen attitude is of a person sitting on the bank of a river facing the water. This person does not turn to right or left, but looks straight ahead, allowing whatever is there to come into consciousness and then to go out of consciousness again. There is no pulling an awareness in nor attempting to hold on as it leaves this moment and another awareness takes its place. Reality comes and goes again in a succession of flowing present time. All that is, is here and now. There is no dichotomy to be found, no judgment. There is no struggle in this place. This flow of life is beyond dichotomy and struggle. Neither is there subject nor object here. There is not what is observed any more than there is an observer. All is one. There is not an inner and an outer and no shifting back and forth; there is only presence. The inner censor, the editor, the divider, the perfectionist, all of whom plague the 8/9/1 in compulsion, are suspended. Self with a small "s" is introduced to Self with a capital "S," the Ground of Being, the reality of Presence.

A mantra chant is often helpful for people in the 8/9/1 triad. Christian liturgical chant can also be significant. Whatever the mantra, its importance is that it becomes a repetitive statement. People in this triad often comment that it is helpful for them to come to that prayer of simple presence so consonant with their incarnation by taking words of a mantra and eliminating them one by one until there remains only silence. A favorite mantra for an 8/9/1 woman I know is: "Be still and know I am God." Using this method, the mantra becomes "Be still and know I am . . . Be still and know I . . . Be still and know . . . Be still . . . Be." The final movement of that mantra is the silence that follows this last word. Again, we see here how a combination of Eastern and Western prayer can blend.

Holy reading, or *lectio divina,* is a tradition that goes back to early Christian monasticism. A combination of holy reading and the use of a mantra provides another blending of Eastern and Western approaches that some 8/9/1s find fruitful. What captures their energy while they are reading is noted. This reading can be Scripture or other literary forms, or the environment, including nature and people. What captures them they choose to retain as a mantra and repeat it over and over again throughout the day. This might be a sentence, the felt sense of a relationship, the look in someone's eyes, the recalling of a cloud pattern. It remains the mantra drawn from a holy reading of some manifestation of the day's life.

The 5/6/7 Triad

For 5/6/7s, it is expanding to the outer and taking that outer inside in a rhythm of breathing that is an aspect of Eastern meditation most useful for them. The quality of the breathing is the important factor here, and pulling that outer in and then releasing it again is the valuable learning in this triad. This is in contrast to their tendency to hold in and to cut their world into small gasps, small pieces, storing it away in a hording manner. Instead, they breathe in and out with rhythmic flow that leads to a place of balance.

Yoga is also helpful for 5/6/7s. In contrast to Zen, which lowers boundaries and opens to all present awareness, the more meditative aspects of yoga involve placing all attention on a seed object until one is drawn into its mystery. The content, then, becomes the focus. Memory, senses, are placed on the one object, one idea, one image, or one symbol. The seed object is tasted and touched, as it were, until the person meditating is swept into the whirlpool of its mystery. What does this do for 5/6/7 people that is uniquely fruitful? It stops the compulsive gathering in of more and more perceptions, bits of information, succeeding possibilities, new ideas or connections. It keeps the perceptual function gently and firmly on a single reality and lets the others fall away.

Another part of the Eastern prayer approach that seems to have good effects for this triad is the use of the *koan*. The koan is a non-rational saying. One of the most famous of these is "What is the sound of one hand clapping?" There is no answer or solution to a koan; one must simply ask and be silent and in the silence yield to the mystery of reality. Life is not a problem with an answer or the key to the solution of a quest. The reminder that life is a mystery is of particular value for 5/6/7s. Though they never stop asking their questions or placing their problems, they need to be reminded that there is no answer to the great realities of life—or the little ones, for that matter—and the koan is that reminder.

The 2/3/4 Triad

The 2/3/4 experience with Eastern prayer forms is one which highlights their body aspects. Hatha yoga can have particular value for people in this triad, but in a different way than for 8/9/1s. This triad tends not to put up boundaries between the physical and the spiritual in their lives. This is an expression of their horizontal spirituality described earlier. For them just being is a blessing, and living itself is holy, as Jewish theologian Abraham Heschel has said.[12] The assuming of the postures or asanas in hatha yoga themselves constitute prayer. The Zen expression that to sit well is to pray well has special significance for 2/3/4s. It also highlights the differing ways the triads look at all of life. Recall that 8/9/1s see hatha yoga as a good preparation for prayer. The distinction made here is between preparation and prayer itself. For 8/9/1s, prayer is something separate and distinct; there is always a boundary of some kind between the spiritual and the non-spiritual for them. In contrast, 2/3/4s speak of hatha yoga as their prayer; moving their body from posture to posture constitutes the prayer.

A woman I know was asked by a group to which she was teaching hatha yoga, what it had taught her, what she had learned from it, and why she practiced it. Her answer surprised even her: "Yoga has taught me to like my body. It has taught me to incorporate my body into all of my living. It has taught me to appreciate all of me." 2/3/4s are taken up with the reality of radical incarnation beyond any categories of secular and spiritual. The spiritual task for them is simply to be human, to live and be and act now. Their own spirit, and therefore the Spirit of Jesus, are united in each moment of life. "I live no longer I, but Christ lives in me"[13] means something very literal to them and includes their entire organism. When they do their hatha yoga and place their bodies in certain postures they express the Spirit of Jesus in this creation. This is the message Eastern prayer forms have for 2/3/4s.

CONTEMPLATIVE LIVING, OUR VOCATION AS HUMAN BEINGS

THE PRAY-ER'S ATTITUDE

The purpose of our becoming pray-ers is to live the contemplative life. We are meant to become contemplatives. While contemplation may sound like a very esoteric experience, in reality it is a characteristically human experience, as I have said before. There are two kinds of contemplation that spiritual masters talk about: active and passive.

Anthony deMello tells the story of the spiritual master who is asked by a disciple what he can do to make himself enlightened. "As little as you can do to make the sun rise in the morning," the master replies. "Then, of what use are the spiritual exercises you prescribe?" the disciple questions. And the master responds, "To make sure you are not asleep when the sun begins to rise."[1] The aspect of contemplation we call active is about staying awake, about not yielding to sleep, about the contribution we can make, and need to make, to our own spiritual journeys. Placing our attention is our contribution toward an experience of contemplation. Spiritual writers of the ages have often called this human contribution active contemplation.

Awareness is a human discipline. Even so, this ability to face reality is a gift from the Divine. We realize this is so when we recall how hard it is to keep our minds from wandering despite our best intentions, or realize how much strength it takes to look life's difficulties in the face. Certainly, for all that we do, we need the power of God. Nevertheless, it is also true that active contemplation depends on our collaboration.

This is in contrast to passive contemplation which surprises us from out of nowhere, as it were. Passive contemplation cannot be programmed. While it is true that our life changes from moment to moment, it is also true that our attitude to that reality can become something of a constant. Acquiring that habit of attention is possibly the main collaboration we can make toward developing a prayer life. We need to be centered, to be waiting for God to nourish our existence. Out of this attitude we meet every moment as it flows past us. Just as we see the current carrying along twigs and pebbles and fish in the stream from our vantage point on the bank, so the content of our life stream changes as we meet moment to moment with focused attention. Awareness of what is so makes us human. It is in this endeavor that we find ourselves. When we do meet ourselves, we can then meet others and God as well.

Such an attitude can be described with the words "awake," "alert," and "relaxed." It is an open-eyed and unflinching gaze that is increasingly honest and entire. While it is frightening to see more and more of what is within and outside ourselves, it is necessary that we do so in the process of living. As we look, we keep growing in courage and risk. We no longer need to be lied to about anything, either by ourselves or others. Our self-deceptions fall away one after another. Less and less do we need to nurture our illusions and delusions, earlier defenses for survival.

Another way to speak about this contemplative attitude, our active contribution to contemplation, is to call it a reading of the book of our life. The book is not some finished volume but a moment by moment new edition. We learn to read this book more thoroughly as we grow in contemplative awareness. We sweep our gaze horizontally over past history, our present situation, our future possibilities, plans, and fears. We also look from the surface of our existence into the depths of it. We experience ourselves in ever richer layers of thought and perception, of emotion, of bodily sensation and response. We especially learn to attend to that kinesthetic sense which indicates the feeling of being "on" or "off." It registers our balance, our sense of ease or dis-ease. It is this interior feeling that things are right with us or that we have pulled up and out of our center that can, when adverted to, be very significant in knowing who we are and what we must do. We call reading that life energy within us "discernment." We call following it, joining its flow, a "wise choice" and a decision for life.

The contemplative attitude can also be said to be synonymous with silence. When we are quiet and truly at rest within ourselves, we see and hear and feel life without defense. The silence I am speaking of here is not the absence of sound. We can be silent in the middle of a crowded city or a classroom, a shouting or laughing family, an office with computers clicking on all sides. The silence I am speaking of is an absence of self, that noisy, created, demanding ego we substitute for the genuine self, the word that we are created to be.

We spend much of our early lives building up an image that we convince ourselves and often others is genuinely us, is who we are. That image contains exaggeration and distortion, lies and deceptions, illusion and delusion. It becomes a god that we must constantly placate because it is greedy to perpetuate itself. When we have a contemplative attitude, however, we move beyond the demands of this created self-image. There we find silence, no excuses, no need to justify, no insistence on looking good. Rather, we honestly admit limitation and weakness.

WHAT THE
CONTEMPLATIVE
ATTITUDE IS NOT

An attitude that is truly contemplative is all of
these things and more. The language of metaphor and imagery serves us well when we try
to talk about it. Sometimes it helps to describe this
receptive openness to life—life with a small "l" and life
with a capital "L"—in terms of what it is not as well as
what it is.

To begin with, there is a trend in contemporary
life toward what many call meditation and its techniques. When these forms began to be popular over

a generation ago, they seemed to promise much to those who made use of them, people looking for inner serenity. It seemed these methods would lead beyond an interior calm to reconciliation among people and mature, selfless interaction. For some, of course, that has been the case. The present interest in living more simply and honestly bears witness to the fact of an increased interest in practice, in genuine spirituality beyond mere rituals and externals.

There are, however, some popular and trendy forms of meditation that are questionable because of their effects in the lives of the individuals and groups that use them. Such so-called meditation is more accurately described as "navel-gazing." This image captures the attitude of self-preoccupation that results from and testifies to inauthentic contemplation; instead of being taken up by the Divine, it is being taken up with me. The outcomes of this so-called contemplation are lack of awareness of genuine personal and social needs and immature self-indulgence.

The proper name for such practice is narcissism masquerading under terms such as prayer, meditation, and contemplation. This practice concentrates on the image we create of ourselves instead of on our real lives, which are always painful to look at in their limitation and poverty, pettiness and ordinariness, in their embarrassing compulsion. Looking at the person beneath the ego's mask brings us to self-confrontation that terrifies, to self-repugnance that disgusts, to our evil which shames us. Eventually, if we can look with courage at what we find, the reflection that removes this mask brings us to humility, which quietly opens us to our deeper selves, our word. We come to know that God has always seen who we are and has accepted us.

Genuine contemplation leads to conversion, to turning upside down who we think we are. We no longer need to talk ourselves into the ego message of seeing ourselves as all-powerful, all-knowing, all-confident; in other words, as god in our lives. From this honesty we are drawn to the poverty and need of others and find a compassion for them, grown out of compassion for ourselves. We accept our creatureliness and the reality of a Creator. Narcissism, on the other hand, lulls us to sleep and demands no change because we find no cause for change. The superficial calming that does not confront reality is what spiritual writers call quietism. Quietism dulls our perceptions, something contemplation never will do, facing us, as it does, with our passionately engaging life experience.

While there is nothing wrong with deliberating, contemplation is not deliberation, either. Weighing and exploring possibilities and options has its place in life, but it is not what I refer to as contemplative activity. Rather, it is mental activity, usually taking place at what the bio-feedback people call the beta level of focused and direct thought. We all, of course, need to deliberate in life; some of us need to be reminded to do so. Some people, however, spend so much time deliberating about each step of their lives that, as Anthony deMello has said, they spend their lives on one leg. Contemplation is a more total activity than deliberation. The entire organism is involved with its functions of feeling and bodily sensation as well as perception. All of who we are responds to the life that comes to us moment by moment.

Knowledge of the Enneagram can show us which of our functions—perceptive, affective, or bodily—is exaggerated. We can see which is downplayed and which mediates between the two. It cannot make us contemplative, but it can reveal our characteristic experience and so teach us who we are. Information about our Enneagram space will not of itself make us pray-ers. Touching our personal lives in self-knowledge and self-remembering can lead us to self-understanding and the self-companioning that finds our spirit together with God's Spirit. Without that depth, the study of the Enneagram is merely another psychological pastime. With it, it becomes what St. Benedict has called a tool of the spiritual craft.[2]

To continue in a similar vein with what contemplation is not, we might note that contemplation is not organized thinking. There are people who spend much time arranging reality in various configurations, connecting it in a myriad of ways. Such mental relating can consume long periods of time in what these people might name prayer or contemplation. Motivation for such activity is often the need to feel safe and secure about reality, to explain and classify it into something manageable and predictable. Information, emotions, persons, one's life history, current events, ideas about the Divine, or forms of prayer are all related to an interior schema. A genuine contemplative attitude has none of this striving for control over ideas which indicates the presence of ego-activity and stands in the way of relaxed flowing with the stream of each successive moment.

While reflecting on our lives can be helpful for us all, it does not constitute the contemplative attitude I am attempting to describe. While reflection can have about it a quality of relaxation, it is still just that: re-flection, bending our gaze back on experience. Contemplation implies being caught up into life right now. We are not next to life observing it. It is true that reflective observations are at times necessary and insightful as preparation for contemplation. Nevertheless, contemplation itself involves all of who we are and leaves nothing outside to critique the experience.

Thomas Merton spoke eloquently about this self-consciousness and self-awareness. He linked it with the false self, with being caught up with image and performance.[3] Anthony deMello describes how when we are truly contemplative we do not know we are, involved as we become with the living of life. Contemplation is experiencing; it is beyond experience being known. It does often happen that our reflections on life, especially reflections on our past history, can draw us into them so that they become present experience. When that happens, we have moved to contemplation. When we remember our childhood with its joys and sorrows, for example, we are reflecting on them. Sometimes, as we do so, we are present again to that happy or sad child. Here and now we live the life of that boy or girl who is no longer merely a memory. Sometimes we finish unfinished and unlived parts of our history in this contemplative way.

Contemplation is not limited to immobility of our bodies either. For some people, contemplation is helped by walking, working, speaking, or singing. The Liturgy of the Hours with its recited and sung psalms and hymns has always contributed to a letting go into life. Those who insist that sitting quietly is essential to contemplation might well consider the story of the master who was accused of always busying himself around his house or traveling afield, and this after speaking about the importance of sitting in contemplation. His response to his accusers was that moving around does not mean that one has ceased sitting in contemplation.[4] This attitude of contemplation is an interior attitude and is affected by inner life, not outer actions.

The contemplative attitude also differs from speculative study. Life cannot just be talked about and looked at from outside. It has to be taken in. We cannot teach anyone the meaning of life and death; every person has to taste life and death for him or her self.

Just as with pudding, speculation will tell us nothing about it; we have to eat it to really know.

Nor is the contemplative life a task or a job. Some people make great efforts to be empty. That is not contemplation; it is work. Contemplation is, however, a discipline of opening our eyes in order to see. It is free of the quality of pushing or even reaching. For example, if we were to breathe on an emerging butterfly, even though we might intend to prepare it to fly by drying it off as it comes out of its cocoon, we would not be helping it at all. In our impatience and unwillingness to wait for its time, we would kill it.[5] So, too, with our contemplative life: we must wait for its time as well.

I have said that active contemplation is the discipline of looking so as not to be asleep when the sun rises, but what do we look at? We look at our lives. We begin at home where God speaks. God always speaks through creation, and so we look at the creation we know best, the one we're closest to, and that creation is ourselves. And so we keep expanding to look at all of our reality. We read and reflect on Scripture, letters that come in the mail, novels and poetry and the daily paper. We read biographies, including our own autobiography, our journal. As we look at our present reality we become conscious of our strengths and our gifts, our deficiencies, especially the one that tells us we must "fill up" our deficiencies.

The greatest lack in us, the one I call our original sin, tells us, as theologian Sebastian Moore says, that we are not desirable as we are.[6] We discover our genuine energies rather than our artificial and contrived ones. We allow, encourage, and enhance those authentic energies by aligning ourselves with them as they flow freely as the stream of our lives. Sometimes we are not correct in distinguishing the hyped, the false, or the merely enthusiastic from those true energies. But we fall on our faces and pick ourselves up; learning is a trial and error phenomenon.

We also pay attention to the neglected aspects of ourselves, those parts that we have downplayed, despised, forgotten, or been frightened by. As we do that, we become aware of which aspects of ourselves we buried. As we attend to our perceptual function, we are aware of the attitudes we have, our reflections, questions, the incongruities we observe out of which we make or see the jokes in life, the funny things. We notice our insights and opinions, the pre-judgments that constitute our prejudices, the superstitions we live from. One major superstition that is common to many people is that when something good happens, something bad will come along soon to spoil things. But there are others as well. We also become aware of our projections, our own issues put on to other people or on to God.

We also learn to pay attention to our feeling function. We become aware of our fears, our rage and resentment, our sorrows and our terrors. We know our anxiety, our enthusiasm, and our despair. We experience our hope, our loneliness, anguish, excitement, infatuations, repulsions, our resistances.

We grow in awareness of our body function including the impressions that come through all of our sensations: sight, hearing, touch, taste, smell, the kinesthetic sense, the sensual enjoyment in our bodies, our genital responses, the feelings of being on or off balance. We experience our feelings of repose, of rest, and of centeredness.

Our lives, of course, are more than just ourselves. They are beyond us, too, and they include other people. We learn increasing awareness of the people we love and those we hate, those we are bored with or indifferent to, those we care for and those who care for us. We deepen our insights into those who are significant to us in one way or another: our family, the different communities of which we are a part, our friends, the men, the women, and the children. We know those who are living, but also those who are deceased; not only people who are ongoing in our day-to-day existence, but also those who are part of our past and who have contributed to who we are now.

We also grow in awareness of what is beyond the individuals in our personal environment. We explore the political and economic situations in our world as well as various cultures and ethnic groups. We deepen our understanding of the problems and issues that face

the world and the people in it today and also the eco-
logical concerns of this planet struggling for survival.

Anthony deMello says it may take us a lifetime
to open our eyes, but seeing comes in a flash. Seeing
always involves a shift, a release, an awareness of incongruities. We move from a childish view that we are the
center of reality to seeing ourselves in a more real perspective. Then we laugh, because perspective always
leads to laughter. We laugh lovingly, not contemptu-
ously, at the joke of our ego-foolishness, at viewing
ourselves at the center of the world.

Who do we see when we gain perspective, when
this shift happens? We see, as the old Chinese Master said, a person riding on an ox, looking for an ox;
somebody who is searching for what is not missing;
somebody climbing a non-existent mountain; a person
striving for contentment; someone dividing the world
in search of unity; someone killing in order to make
peace in the world; somebody working hard for grace,
which is by definition gift; someone who creates alien-
ation so people can come together; someone questing
for God when they really are already standing on
sacred ground. When we look we see God already in
our lives; we do not have to put God there.

All of this might be described as active contemplation. What, then, is passive contemplation? First of all,
it is something we do not bring about. We do change,
but not as a result of our endeavors and efforts. We
are different, but we do not make ourselves that way.

Transformation or conversion, according to deMello's Master, is not the consequence of something done but of something dropped. Yet, not even the dropping of something is ours to do. The process of living strips away the illusions and delusions of our lives, which can no longer deceive us. Living our lives shows us who we are. People around us tell us, circumstances demand our response. In the process of conversion and transformation we make peace with the incarnation we are as Jesus did, the Incarnate One, the Wise One, who embraced humanity. When we live consciously, life flows through us. Less and less we hold it off. Is not the very living of our human life itself the deepest union with Fullness of Life that we can experience? And did Jesus not say, "I am . . . the life"?[7]

Once again, how can the Enneagram help us with all this? To study the Enneagram is a very helpful prelude to becoming a more aware and sensitive human instrument in creation, someone through whom life/ Life can flow. We become more aware through the Enneagram of what our dynamics are. What are the themes that re-occur in my experience because of who I am? A genuine understanding and appreciation of the Enneagram demands that one be on the journey. We need to be seeking life in order to approach the Enneagram intelligently. We must be willing to ask the questions and receive the answers more and more from our experience: How do I frustrate myself? What clouds my perceptions? What blocks the flow of my energy? What paralyzes me? What sends me into compulsive, automatic, addictive stimulus and response? What is natural to me? What can assist me? What can captivate my energies for growth? What is my unique gift?

The Enneagram is a tool on life's journey that shows us how we can—and how we do—make ourselves the enemy of who we are capable of being. It introduces us to ourselves more and more and aids us in our friendship with and understanding of ourselves. This is the prerequisite for openness and compassion toward others. The Enneagram allows us increasingly to let in the reality we learn early in life to deny. It enables us to go beyond narcissistic navel-gazing to the self-confrontation that leads us to the humble word we are meant to be.

The Enneagram provides an atmosphere in which we can be taken up and taken over by life/Life. As this happens, we are also helped to observe, listen to, and understand other people from their various vantage points, outlooks, and stances different from our own. These awarenesses lead to patience and demand humor. They require that we reveal ourselves so that others can know where we are coming from. They involve the admission of our limitations, knowing that neither ourselves nor others have all of life experience at our disposal.

As we accept and forgive and are reconciled with the limitations in us, we become more reconciled with and allowing for those limitations in others. We are more able to forgive the human frailty, the creatureliness, we see in ourselves and in others. We become more accepting persons of all who share in the human condition. We grow in the ability to communicate ourselves to others and receive communication from them. Our defensiveness and resistance toward our own and others' reality lessens. Boundaries gradually melt away and we become persons of love, unity, and oneness. We flow ever more with all of creation. We increasingly are living pray-ers, living prayers. We become the contemplatives that all conscious human beings are meant to be, and in doing so fulfill our destiny. Of course, all of this can happen whether or not we have ever heard of the Enneagram. Nevertheless, the description this approach offers of our giftedness and our sabotage of that giftedness, can serve as a powerful help along our Way.

NOTES

Introduction

1. Thomas Merton, *The Springs of Contemplation* (New York: Farrar, Straus & Giroux, 1992). This book incorporates Merton's mature expression of the life of prayer and spirituality.
2. Piero Ferrucci, *What we May Be* (Los Angeles: Houghton Mifflin, 1982), p. 33.
3. Mary Luke Tobin, S.L. "Merton on Prayer: Start Where You Are," National Catholic Reporter, *Praying Supplement #1.*
4. *The Rule of St. Benedict* (Collegeville, MN: The Liturgical Press, 1981). The Prologue.

5. Suzanne Zuercher, O.S.B., *Enneagram Spirituality: From Compulsion to Contemplation* (Notre Dame, IN: Ave Maria Press, 1992); *Enneagram Companions; Relationship and Spiritual Direction* (Suzanne Zuercher, O.S.B., 2000), and *Merton, An Enneagram Profile* (Suzanne Zuercher, O.S.B., 2001). The latter two books are available through Ingram Publishers. In recent years I have found two authors who take the study of the Enneagram to new depths of spirituality. These are A.H. Almaas (*Facets of Unity,* Berkeley, CA: Diamond Books, 1998) and Sandra Maitri (*The Spiritual Dimension of the Enneagram*, New York: Jeremy P. Tarcher/Putnam, 2000, and *The Enneagram of Passions and Virtues*, New York: Jeremy P. Tarcher/Penguin, 2005.)

Approaches to the Interior Life

1. Teresa of Avila, *The Interior Castle*, trans. By Kieran Kavanaugh and Otilio Rodriguez (New York: Paulist Press, 1979).

2. Anthony de Mello, *Awareness* (New York: Doubleday, 1990 by the Center for Spiritual Exchange). This book is a verbatim account of the author's conferences on the spiritual life and demonstrates a major theme in his writings: We need to simply live rather than analyzing our experience.

3. Karlfried Graf von Durckheim, *The Way of Transformation* (London: George Allen and Unwin, 1985), "Everyday Life as Practice."

4. David Steindl-Rast, *Gratefulness, the Heart of Prayer* (NewYork: Paulist Press, 1984), p. 135.

5. There are several summaries of Merton's writings on prayer. Three of my favorites are *Merton's Palace of Nowhere* by James Finley (Notre Dame, IN: Ave Maria Press, 1978); *Thomas Merton's Dark Path* by William H. Shannon (Dallas, PA: Offset Paperback Mfrs., Inc., 1982); and *A Search for Wisdom and Spirit* by Anne E. Carr (Notre Dame, IN: University of Notre Dame Press, 1988.)

6. Sam Keen, *The Passionate Life* (New York: Harper and Row, 1983), "The Outlaw."

Methods in the Life of Prayer

1. For a full development of his approach, see *Focusing* by Eugene Gendlin (New York: Everest House, 1978).

2. The Book of Psalms in the Bible contains many passages about revealing one's self to God.

3. See the discussion of the primary, auxiliary, and buried functions of each triad in my books.

4. Steindl-Rast, *Gratefulness, the Heart of Prayer,* p. 133.

5. I suggest a reading of Sam Keen's books as a way to see how one contemporary person has responded to the call to transformation.

6. An overview of Thomas Merton's life as told in his journals is found in *The Intimate Merton*, edited by Patrick Hart and Jonathan Montaldo (New York: Harper Collins, 1999).

7. Rainer Maria Rilke, *Letters to a Young Poet* (New York: W.W. Norton, 1993).

8. An extensive bibliography of dream theory can be found in the book *Dream Work* by Jeremy Taylor (New York/Ramsey, NJ: Paulist Press, 1983).

9. This example is from a taped workshop given in Pecos, New Mexico, by Johnson.

10. Matthew 26:26.

11. Merton wrote extensively on this East/West spiritual interchange. One example of this is the book *Zen and the Birds of Appetite* (New York: New Directions, 1968).

12. Richard Seidman, *The Oracle of Kabbalah: Mystical Teachings of the Hebrew Letters* (New York: Thomas Dunne Books, 2001) p.141.

13. Galatians 2:20.

Contemplative Living, Our Vocation as Human Beings

1. Anthony de Mello, *One Minute Wisdom* (Garden City, NY: Doubleday and Company, Inc., 1986), p. 11. This book, with its stories of Master and Disciple, is the source of many of the ideas in this discussion about contemplation.

2. *The Rule of St. Benedict,* Chapter 4, "The Instruments of Good Works."

3. For an insightful articulation of Merton's writings on the true and false self I recommend *Merton's Palace of Nowhere* (Notre Dame, IN: Ave Maria Press, 1978), James Finley's classic on the subject.

4. de Mello, *One Minute Wisdom*, p. 157.

5. de Mello, *One Minute Wisdom*, p. 167.

6. In his book, *The Crucified Jesus is no Stranger*, theologian, poet, and Benedictine monk Sebastian Moore describes how we put to death the Christ life within us.

7. John 14:6.

Suzanne Zuercher, O.S.B., is a member of the Benedictine Sisters of Chicago. She is a pioneer in the spirituality of the Enneagram and has presented workshops and programs on the subject around the world.

AVE MARIA PRESS

Founded in 1865, Ave Maria Press,
a ministry of the Congregation of
Holy Cross, is a Catholic publishing
company that serves the spiritual and
formative needs of the Church and its
schools, institutions, and ministers;
Christian individuals and families; and
others seeking spiritual nourishment.

For a complete listing of titles from

Ave Maria Press

Sorin Books

Forest of Peace

Christian Classics

visit www.avemariapress.com

AVE MARIA PRESS
Notre Dame, IN
A Ministry of the United States Province of Holy Cross